I Finished High School.
Now What?

Stacey McCrory

WESTBOW
PRESS®
A DIVISION OF THOMAS NELSON
& ZONDERVAN

WestBow Press books may be ordered through booksellers or by contacting:

WestBow Press
A Division of Thomas Nelson & Zondervan
1663 Liberty Drive
Bloomington, IN 47403
www.westbowpress.com
1 (866) 928-1240

ISBN: 978-1-9736-5763-7 (sc)
ISBN: 978-1-9736-5764-4 (hc)
ISBN: 978-1-9736-5762-0 (e)

Library of Congress Control Number: 2019904386

Print information available on the last page.

WestBow Press rev. date: 5/16/2019

For all the college students at Crossroads Baptist Church. These past seven years have been so amazing getting to know each one of you and watching you grow. Michael and I love you very much and think of you as one of our own. We know that your future is so important for God's kingdom, and we want to see you be successful in all you do.

Thank you so much to my husband and to all my children. You are my inspiration! I love you!

Contents

Preface

This book is more than just practical advice. It's about real life and the struggles we all face. It's about the things we either don't know or didn't think to ask about. Your parents can't teach you everything, and some things have never been second nature for you; however, you can learn. The knowledge you will gain from the information in this book will also teach you some life skills. Someone else has made all the mistakes and struggled for you so that you don't have to. These details are written down here so that you can start with an advantage. You won't think to yourself in the future, If I only knew then what I know now.

As we grow older, our thinking becomes more mature, and we start to enjoy different activities. What we used to think of as fun isn't so much fun any longer. As we change, our attitudes and ways of thinking change with us. Here's a scripture about growing into an adult that comes to mind. "When I was a child, I spoke like a child, I thought like a child, I reasoned like a child. When I became a man, I gave up childish ways" (1 Corinthians 13:11 NIV).

You will have so many questions about what decisions to make when it comes to college, your career, or other life choices (e.g., credit, buying a home, saving money, needing relationship advice). In this book we talk about all these things and more in detail. The Bible is one book that has teaching on work ethics, life choices, stewardship, and relationships. You will see scripture references throughout this book used to back up the advice along with practical guidance based on people's personal experiences in each chapter.

I know what it feels like to be as lost as a goose and trying to make the best decisions. This is the most important time in your life and can alter your life's direction forever. One NewsNow report divulged that roughly 70 percent of Christian college students going off to college end up leaving their faith during their first year on campus. This is one statistic I would like to see much lower. My heart goes out to this age group. There are so many changes right now, and they have many decisions to make. I saw a need for a book with biblical perspective and godly advice to help this age group understand that the choices they are making now have consequences and far-reaching results. You must take life and yourself serious in your endeavors. You must be focused and not scattered, running around aimlessly like a chicken with your head cut off. If you had someone to help you look at your options and tell you what you are getting yourself into, it would make life so much easier. That is what I have tried to do here—to give you all the details in one place so you can succeed at the start and not muddle your way through it.

The Heart of
the Matter

As you wind down your senior year in high school, there is so much excitement in the air, so much to consider, and lots of decisions being made. Have you decided to go to college? Maybe you have decided to work in a position that doesn't require a college degree. Some careers are based on skill, aptitude, or hands-on training. Where are you thinking about living? Will you live at home, rent a place, or live in the dorms? Have you sat down with a pen and paper to see what you can afford? Will you stay in your hometown, or are you feeling God leading you somewhere else?

In this book of practical advice, we will discuss these and many more important life-altering questions. You will learn how to make every decision count and how to research in a smart way. This book will address both college-bound and work-bound students. How do you navigate each of these avenues? It's like you step off the graduation stage, and then you are thrown into this whole new world! After high school, you will be moving forward and growing in your maturity in so many aspects of life. Embrace these changes. Change is not always a bad thing. It is only a momentary season that's intended to grow you, and it opens you up to a world of opportunity. What you do with those opportunities and the way you respond to change will ultimately direct your life path. Remembering your school days and memories are wonderful unless you get stuck in the past. The past is past for a reason. Learn from it, and move forward.

Have you ever said to yourself, "Why didn't someone tell me that?" Well, now you have the tell-all book in your hands! Topics range from professional advice to practical application. These are the answers to the questions you never knew to ask!

STACEY MCCRORY

These are details no one thinks about telling you. Sure, you may get some information from one person and another piece of information from another, but this is an all-in-one guide to navigate life after you graduate.

Flashback!

You have been zoning out and daydreaming about what life would be like after you graduated. You have dreamed of being successful at your job and working for a great company. You can just picture yourself having the life you've always dreamed of. In your mind, you have it all figured out, and you are excited to get started on this journey.

On graduation day you think to yourself, *This is it! Finally, the day I have been looking forward to—the day I've been dreaming about for years! No more early mornings, eating cafeteria food, or sitting all day at a desk. The desk was very constricting, very cold, and hard, and most of the teachers were so boring. Blah, blah, blah all day long.* Of course, there were a few favorites just like any school has. Mr. Morgan was everyone's favorite teacher. He had been confined to a wheelchair for life, but no one treated him any differently because everyone just loved him.

Sure, there will be things you are going to miss about those high school days, but you have been dreaming about graduating for as long as you can remember. With each year that passed came excitement along with more and more reality sinking in. You likely wrote down all your plans and collected your own stuff, including dishes, pots, and pans. It took lots and lots of researching. Are you really ready to live on your own away from Mom and Dad, or will you stay awhile to save some money?

For example, some college-bound students decide to commute back and forth to college from home, and some live on or near campus. Living at home is smart if you can get along with your family. However, some aren't that lucky, and they just have to be strong and do it on their own, determined to make it no matter what they will face ahead. Either they don't want to be burdens on their parents anymore, or they just can't stand the fact of living under the same roof with them any longer. They feel they will suffocate and never get anywhere in life if they stay there.

You may want to move out and go away to college to experience life or to be able to live away from home. Right now you still have the option of going back and living at home if you get in a bind and don't make it on your own. Can you make it on your own without your parents? No one has the answer to that question except for you. You do have to count the cost. You must sit down with a pen and paper to calculate all the bills each month. No matter what you think, most parents will let you come back home. Your parents will likely be happy to have you back, and you may have just changed your mind. Whatever decision it is, make sure to do it for yourself and not for anything or anyone else.

College-bound students with parents who have gone to college tend to have some perspective on their life paths. Those students have reaped the benefits of their parents' life choices. They have a leg up. Those of you with scholarships for ACT test scores, high school GPAs, and sports-related activities will get much-needed financial relief. Some of us—maybe you—can't afford college, and neither can your parents. You have to depend on grants or student loans to carry you through college.

You may not have had role models or mentors to educate you and guide you down a certain path, and life is about as clear as mud. The truth is that you can't thrive without the help of someone educating you in this world. But you must have a desire to succeed inside of you. You must want it! The good news is that the Bible tells us that if we work, we will make a profit, and sleeping or yapping all the time will put you in the poorhouse! Think about this saying: Where there is a will, there is a way.

Once you are educated on the ins and outs and have the know-how, you learn there are ways to go to college without a bank account full of money—and without the help of family. Maybe there's a grant or a loan out there to help you pay for school. If you have already chosen a college, that is great! If you are still deciding, there is still time. Then again, college may not be for you, and you may not be thinking along those lines. Maybe you have a skill that allows you to go right into a career without a degree. We will talk more in detail about this in a later chapter.

> When considering loans, you should borrow only what is necessary over and above your free grants. Using your loans to live on is not a good idea.

In some situations your mom or dad have no idea how to help you consider going to college because they never went to college and wouldn't know where to start. You will find out that you must learn many things in this life on your own. It's definitely going to require work and determination along with asking plenty of questions. Here's a good piece of advice: Surround yourself with people who are where you want to be. That is a great habit you could start today. You can keep close to friends of your family, past teachers, counselors, business owners, friends at church, and so many more individuals who will allow you the opportunity to ask questions and learn from them.

Successful people are successful because they have been there and have failed more times than they have succeeded and learned from their failures. They have made a lot of mistakes, and they have learned from those mistakes. Successful adults have had mentors, pastors, or youth leaders who cared enough to educate and encourage them along the way. However, knowing you want to be successful and achieving success are two totally different types of mind-sets. One is your dreams, and one is your persistence and consistency along with the knowledge you've learned along the way. For example, you can dream about being a restaurant owner for most of your life; however, once you graduate high school, your thought process changes, and that changes your dreams too. Sometimes circumstances can change and cause a ripple in the pond and a change in your dreams and goals.

If you go to church, you may have heard this scripture: "Though a righteous man falls seven times, he will get up, but the wicked will stumble into ruin" (Proverbs 24:16 NIV).

Never give up. Try and try again. Be persistent in your pursuits with patience and consistency. God blesses those who pursue His righteousness. Think about your big decisions and long-term goals long and hard. You may realize that your dream will have to be a dream come true sometime down the road, or you may never realize that dream. It may not be the right time, and you don't have all the resources available to start. More importantly, if you're not putting God first in life, that will make your life and path harder. God guides you through with His Holy

Spirit and will show you open doors that He has set before you. He will also close some doors that aren't meant to be opened. It's important to have a relationship with Him. His Holy Spirit will help you discern right from wrong and know what His will is for your life. With that said, the devil can also get in your head and tell you lies that beat you down mentally and discourage you. Remember nothing is impossible with God. The Bible tells us anything is possible, but not everything is beneficial.

Diving Deeper

Everything in life flows from the heart. If you're already a believer in Christ and have read His Word, you know He asks every believer to love Him with all our hearts, minds, and souls. You should put Him first in every decision. Totally devote and surrender yourself to Him and His will. This means letting Him guide you through your life and the plans that He has for you. His plans include an abundant life for you. He will work things together for our good.

> And a ruler asked him, "Good Teacher, what must I do to inherit eternal life:" And Jesus said to him, "Why do you call me good? No one is good except God alone. You know the commandments: Do not commit adultery, Do not murder, Do not steal, Do not bear false witness, Honor your father and mother." And he said, "All these I have kept from my youth." When Jesus heard this, he said to him, "One thing you still lack. Sell all that you have and distribute to the poor, and you will have treasure in heaven; and come, follow me." But when he heard these things, he became very sad, for he was extremely rich. (Luke 18:18–23 NIV)

Look at the scripture in Luke of the rich young ruler. Is there just one thing that is holding you back from fully surrendering to God? Is it that one thing you just can't let go of? It has such a stronghold on you that you have no idea how to even start without it. In the Bible, God calls this covetousness and states that covetousness and idolatry go hand in hand. You are choosing to put something else in God's place, putting it first in your life. Life is about choices, and God gives you the freedom to make your own choices or decisions, which is called free will. Your heart is involved in most of the decisions you will make. The rich young ruler decided that he could not put God over the one thing he loved the most, specifically his vast wealth. You need to be willing to give it all to Christ and make Him your number-one priority over any and everything else. You are His number-one priority. He loves you so much and has a purpose specifically for you that He set in motion before you were even in your mother's womb. Always remember that God has a time and a season for His purpose. Everything happens for a reason. It's not always immediately shown to you, and it's not always in your time; however, know His timing is perfect. By putting Him first, everything else will fall into line. He wants to be part of how your life turns out if you let Him. However, you play a part in how this life turns out with faith and action. He will not do it for you, but He will be right there with you.

Your plans are going to change, and your circumstances will change, sometimes in the most unexpected ways. You may be stuck in that job just a There is a time for everything and a season for every activity under the heavens (Ecclesiastes 3:1 NIV).

little longer until another door opens. Don't try to force it open if it's closed! If it is in God's plan, you will find that He will give you peace about those decisions. It's tempting for us to get involved and try to take control, but God's plan is better. You will find that our choices and decisions tend to go more smoothly when God's involved instead of mass chaos when Satan is involved.

However, just because you are hitting brick walls, that doesn't always mean that it's the devil's work. It could be God protecting you. Sometimes bad things happen to good people, and you are not given the foresight to see what is at work and for what purpose. Consider Job in the Old Testament. You can see now exactly what was going on because someone wrote it down for us. Job didn't have that same foresight and had to have faith and trust God. In the book of Job, you find God must give permission to Satan to take certain actions. So too, the chaos could just be the result of our sinful and fallen state. When we make decisions, there are consequences to those decisions.

Sometimes you may fall off into a pothole because you zigged when you should have zagged, right? Living in a sinful world in this flesh is going to make you susceptible to sin, and you may fall prey to bad decisions. Life is a spiritual battle, even though you live in the flesh. Keep this in mind when you are going about your daily

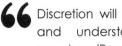 Discretion will protect you, and understanding will guard you (Proverbs 2:11 NIV).

routines. For example, next time you get behind that one slow poke on the road when you are in a hurry, hang back. Don't be tempted to pass the person so quickly. Relax. You are not going to make it to your destination any faster. You think you will, but then you look up and see the car you just passed pull up next to you at the next red light. It could very well be that God is keeping you from becoming involved in an accident that is going to happen up the road. Have you ever thought of it that way?

Have you ever wondered why sometimes you just can't seem to get out the door? Why do things keep going wrong, or why can't you do anything right? Have you thought that maybe you are being refined? Maybe your faith is being tested. You may think to yourself, *What kind of decisions have I made, and are they the right ones? I don't want to be in school for the rest of my life. What if I fail?* It's good to think about these things.

What would you do if you didn't go to college? What would your life be like in a couple of years, and how would you reach your goals? Is there an easier way to know exactly what you're supposed to do, and how long it will take? Will the road you take be an easy one?

You are responsible for yourself, and now is the opportunity to take on more of this responsibility. You could possibly end up putting yourself at a disadvantage by not learning to do something by yourself. Why not learn how to do it on your own and have the knowledge and feeling of accomplishment. You will be surprised just how much you can do on your own if you only try to apply yourself. More times than not, it takes less time to do something yourself than waiting for someone else to do it for you.

Priorities and Church

How does this scripture and God relate to priorities? Life is about making decision after decision, and how we prioritize those decisions will direct our days, months, and   Whoever pursues righteous and kindness, will find life, righteousness, and honor (Proverbs 21:21 NIV).

even years. Who we let influence these priorities is also just as important.

One decision you may be contemplating is if you will continue to go to church. Will you keep going to your home church, or will you look at other churches near you? You come from a small church that doesn't offer a college and career class option, and you don't feel like you fit in with the adult Sunday school classes.

Your parents go to church. You have friends who go to church, and you love to hang out with everyone. Sure, since you've graduated, things have been laxer, and you may have even gotten a little lazy about going. You're at school or just plain exhausted, and so you tell yourself, "I'll just go to Sunday school instead of big church." But you know deep down inside that there is a good chance you won't even make it to church at all.

As time goes on, other thoughts start to run through your head. *It's time for some me time. I deserve it! I have no responsibilities, nowhere to be.* You just need a break for a while. To be honest, you really don't care. You have been working so hard and have been in school for so long—practically all of your life—so you feel you deserve to stop and just do nothing for a while. You know deep down that this kind of thinking will set you up for many missed opportunities to grow and become the person God intends you to be. If you're not careful, you will talk yourself right out of going to church at all, and you could very possibly end up falling away from the Lord.

What if you're the person reading this and you think, *I didn't go to church in the first place. This doesn't apply to me. Why do people think this is so important?* Well, today is a good day to ask yourself why you don't go. If you don't know much about God, Jesus, or church, ask some friends. In fact, go with them for a visit. You can even try several local churches to see what everyone is talking about. How do you know what you believe if you have never given church a chance or have never heard what God may have to say to you personally? God does have a purpose for your life and wants to be a part of it. He does have something to say specifically to you. Will you give Him the chance to show you His love?

This is the time in your life when you are going to have so much thrown your way, and you must start thinking responsibly and get out of your high school thinking and shift over to thinking like an adult and taking on new priorities. Now is the time to get serious. You have graduated, and you're ready for the next chapter. There is a world of opportunities out there, and you feel like you can conquer the world. You have waited your entire life to be respected and treated like a grown adult. Well, here is your chance. You've done it. Now what?

This Thing
Called Adulting

Adulting is basically having responsibility and faking it till you make it. It doesn't come naturally. It comes as you learn, grow, and see examples of other adults who have figured it out already.

You may be thinking, *So what's the big deal? This is going to be a piece of cake! I've got this all figured out. I know where I want to go and what I want to accomplish. At least I think I do, and I'm pretty sure I know how I'm going to get there.*

But wait! How do I find out information about things if I can't ask my parents? How do I buy my groceries? Do I buy them just once a week? Where do I pay my bills? These decisions are going to stress you out at first until you get your own rhythm down. Your own personality and ways of doing things will come through, and you will get into your own routine. With a little help, you will find your groove. Stress is always a part of life, and it seems to multiply when you are bombarded by all new decisions. Everyone goes through this. You're not alone.

For example, one adulting decision is how you do your grocery shopping, whether you buy them once a week or more often. You may want to start saving some recipes or go buy a small cookbook to start experimenting with your cooking and baking style. So building a grocery list when you run out of things may be a great idea. Some are naturally better cooks than bakers and vice versa. Don't let this frustrate you. Cooking skills come with practice and time. When it comes to doing laundry, it may also be easier to wash

> But I tell you that everyone will have to give an account for every empty word they have spoken (Matthew 12:36 NIV).

STACEY MCCRORY

clothes once a week or a few times a week to stay on top of it. You will learn by trial and error and find out what works best for you.

This is one of the most crucial times of your life as you grow into adulthood. The decisions and choices you make now will haunt you, hinder you, or enable you so that you grow toward your future self. Be careful of your choices because they do matter, and they do have consequences, good and bad, big and small. You're creating lifelong habits, and your decisions have eternal consequences too.

Navigating Adult Life as a Christian

So what am I going to do, and how am I going to do it? Lots of you have this type of question, even if you have laid your foundation and have a basic plan in place. Always start with writing down your goals and your starting point, and you will have your initial plan. You may even have a five-year plan, but for now, let's start with some basics and go from there.

It's okay if you don't have it all figured out yet! You are not supposed to, not at this point in your life anyway. Things can change so unexpectedly and will alter your plans, sometimes forever. If you pray and listen to God, you can ask Him to show you His purpose for your life. We all have God-given talents and gifts from the Holy Spirit. We only need to be tuned into the Spirit to hear and see His plan. How will you have an intimate relationship with Jesus and be led by the Spirit unless you pray and seek His will? It all starts by prayer, diving into His Word and taking it to heart. His Word is the truth, no matter what anyone else tells you. The Word gives every possible solution to every possible scenario and situation. People in general are the ones who make navigating life complicated. Use His Word to help you navigate everything you do.

Let me tell you about a girl named Sarah, who had a plan to sit out of college the first year and then go the next year for her basics. She got a job at a fast-food restaurant close to where she was living. Then before that year was even up, she changed her mind about school. She started touring colleges and got excited about starting, and so she started her paperwork for her financial aid and grants. After starting school, she decided to get a low-income apartment so that she could live totally on her own instead of with family. She started school with nineteen hours. She was working forty hours a week at a restaurant and twenty-four hours a week at a grocery store. The whole time she was in school, she partied on the weekends. She thought she was superwoman and could do it all. She wanted to live on her own, work, pay the bills, pass school, and party. It wasn't until the end of the first semester when she saw her 1.75 GPA that she realized she needed to get serious about school and cut out some things. Talk about a wake-up call! Try not to overload yourself the first year until you see how you will handle everything.

By keeping your mind grounded in God's Word, it lives through you. God will be active in your life and affect how you're living. You're going to have the ability to look from the outside with eyes wide open to see the corruption and twisted lies that this world would have you believe. The apostle John reminds us in the scripture that Gods Word is living and breathing in us. Sarah didn't have God in her life at all during that time, and her train came off the rails. She couldn't see the forest for the trees.

As Christians and followers of Jesus, we are aliens here on earth. We are not of this world because we have been adopted as sons and daughters of King Jesus, and we are residents of an eternal kingdom with Him. This world's ways make us long more for our forever home because we are called to be different and set apart. The customs and beliefs of most the world are so wacky that we wonder how everyone else can be blinded by all the craziness that goes on. How can they not see what is going on here? We are blinded by our own blindness. The Bible tells us, "Their minds have been blinded, because of their unbelieving and unrepentant heart." They become lovers of evil and cannot see that they are doing anything wrong. After all, everyone else is doing it. It's just the norm.

Who or what are you letting control your life? This world and the devil pull us toward sin. If we are not grounded in God's Word and if we are not careful, the devil can take control and pull our lives down. Sarah got caught up in the world and lost her focus, and because she lost her focus, things started to spin out of control within only one year. She had so much going on at once that her focus wasn't on God but on the worldly things. You can break free from the chains of bondage that the things of this world have on you. If everyone else jumped off a thirty-story building, would you? That's my point exactly! My mom used to say that to me all the time. We are not supposed to be conformed to this world. We are a new creation. We shouldn't fold to peer pressure and the lie Satan is telling us just because everyone else is doing it. Really think about your actions. Are you going to sit there and be a puppet on a string and let them dictate what you do? You are your own person, and you have the strength through Christ Jesus to walk away and make a different choice. Try it and see. I dare you! Just see if you ever go back to your so-called friends who are just barely acquaintances and who will ultimately ditch you for their next followers. Be a leader, not a follower. If someone doesn't want to be your friend, shake the dust off your shoes and move on. They were not your friends in the first place.

Peer pressure is allowing another person or people to wield influence over you and persuade you to do things you wouldn't normally do. These people are just grown-up bullies! You are not their servant, and you don't have to do everything they suggest. You can say no. You could say they are hypocrites just like the Pharisees, the religious leaders of the Lord's day. The Pharisees were always trying to trip Jesus up or trap Him with their questions, not understanding that He was the promised Messiah who was foretold by the prophets hundreds of years beforehand. Oh, if they had only known what we do now. We see the same thing with people and the herd mentality. Decide to be your best self, not a follower of who knows what. You are the navigator here, and God is your guide.

You will come to find out for yourself that people will test you and try to trip you up on your beliefs and question your decisions. Be sure you know what you believe and why you believe it. That way, you can defend your faith and maybe even plant a seed in their lives. You could be part of God's plan, which is orchestrated by His hand, to draw this person to Him and the promise of God didn't really say you would surely die, did He? (Genesis 3:1–12 NIV). eternal life. The most practiced sin in the world all started with the first sin—a lie.

STACEY MCCRORY

The devil is still planting the same type question in your mind. Your non-Christian and Christian friends will ask you to violate your conscience, to make an exception just this once. It all seems so innocent, and besides, these are your friends. They wouldn't lead you wrong. However, if you feel the Holy Spirit convicting you and telling you, "No, danger, danger," then listen to that voice. This is what the Bible calls discernment from the Holy Spirit, and it's meant to protect you. It's kind of like your conscience. It's there to make you think twice before acting. It runs the caution flag up the pole. You will learn even more about this as you age.

The Bible tells us that the devil prowls around to deceive us and lead us into a life that leads to death. Life's a spiritual battle, and we need to wear God's full armor to protect us. Watching for pride and keeping your inner voice in check will teach you self-control. Adam and Eve didn't, and both were deceived, which led to shame and them hiding from God. Why worry about pride? We don't like to be told we can't do something. We don't like to think something is out of our reach and we can't have it. This is a prime example of what your mama always told you, "You can't always have everything you want."

Your personal impact on other people's lives is something that is hard to calculate. However, it extends far beyond your fingertips. Someone is always going to be watching you—God, other people, social media, etc. We have no idea of our impact on people. Think about just one person or a group and how they can affect society. Choose to be the bigger person and do the right thing and make the right choice. There are plenty of examples in history of one person who changed the direction of the whole world by making that one decision. It all starts with just one person, and that person can cause a ripple effect that will carry on for generations. Be careful, be mindful, and be thoughtful. You can make a difference for your generation.

"Christianity is only one generation away from extinction," said the former archbishop of Canterbury Lord Carey.

Not Considering College?

How will you get from point A to point B in life if you don't go to college and speak Logistics is "the management of the details of an operation" (freedictionary.com). to a counselor? How do you manage logistics of your life and choose roads wisely if you have never done it before? Figuring out the logistics is part of navigating life as an adult after high school.

So let's discuss the possibility of careers without college. There are limitless possibilities available. If we were to think back to the example of Sarah and fast-forward a few years, we would find Sarah trying to decide if she wants to stay in college or find a good job somewhere. She doesn't want to disappoint her family, and she doesn't want to feel like a failure. So which way does she choose? Which is the right road for her to travel down? When it comes to decisions, it can really make your head spin. Right now is the best time to explore all possible options and opportunities while you're young. The only thing standing in your way is you. You can do anything you put your mind to. It is going to be stressful at first. But stay focused, and you can do it.

So let's use an example scenario to see how this could play out. Your friend's dad works at a life insurance company as a manager and offers you an opportunity to double your current pay. Sounds pretty good, right? In addition, you can get out of blue-collar work and into a white-collar job with room to grow. You'll have a job where the income potential is only limited by you and your drive. You already have two years of community college under your belt. You had a plan and goal of becoming a radiologist. A university board has met with you and thought it would be a good idea for you to complete basic prerequisites at a junior college first before coming into the university program. You trust their professional counsel and go in that direction, but something in you says that this may not be the field for you. So you tell yourself you will be a nurse just like your mom is. She thinks you would do great, and you can see on her face that she would be so proud of you. Why not? You have been fascinated by hospitals since you were young, especially since you were in and out of them enough. The nurses were always so sweet, and besides, you only have to check on patients, take their temperature, give shots, and socialize, right? Wrong, wrong, wrong! There is always so much more that goes on behind the scenes that you don't see. The everyday visitor or patient is not going to see everything that goes on, and a lot of the nurse's work is unseen. During a shift you may have to change a diaper, put in an IV, give CPR, or assist in surgery. There is going to be charting, getting medicine ready, and monitoring vitals. There are lots of situations that could arise, and you really have to be sharp, educated, and able to respond quickly and correctly in a time of crisis. There are some perks though, including the salary, overtime, and shift differential. Plus traveling nurses can visit different cities, and along with the job comes the prestige of the title and a good living. Some nurses—a nurse anesthetist for example gets five weeks of vacation per year. Yowza! What a perk! Just be sure you think before you leap! Make sure that your decision is based on the right reasons and that it's a profession that you will enjoy in the long term. You should know all the pros and cons of the job. Never choose a profession based on salary alone. There is much to be said about really enjoying where you work and who you work for and with.

Thinking logically, you know money isn't everything, and you don't know if you will be able to give shots, take patients to the toilet, or give them baths! The truth is that you can do anything with practice and determination. The sky is the limit. You just need to step out in faith. Again, think about your motivation, and ask yourself if you have the desire to do this type of job. Determine what is important and what work you could be happy doing and go for it!

People will tell you, "oh, you don't want to do that!" Or they will say, "You can't do that." Then, of course, you will always encounter the Negative Nellies. It may seem like moms and family members always put in their two cents and that they can be the worst offenders. Consider this though: Your family does know you best, and they do have your best interest at heart. They may give you an idea you haven't considered, so hear them out before shutting them down. Be sure you are asking the right people for advice. Use discernment when you talk to people, and listen to advice from those who are where you want to be now. If you wanted to be an attorney, you wouldn't go ask advice from a doctor. This is what you must consider when seeking advice on your career choices. Remember those looking from the outside in have a unique perspective that you don't have.

Only you know what you are capable of, so don't let anyone limit your potential. But don't forgo seeking sound advice either. When I say sound, I mean someone who has been where you want to go, someone who is more educated than you, someone who is in that occupation or business right now such as an adult or graduate. People love to talk about themselves and their experiences. Some will share more than others, and that's okay. Take whatever wisdom they give you, and write it down.

> **Always gather as much information as possible, and never stop asking questions. You will never know it all. Everyone has different perspectives.**

Now let's consider the insurance job that your friend's dad offered you. You take the job, and you go in guns blazing, kicking tail, and taking down names. Let's say you work there for two years. You were rookie of the month the second month in, even exceeding the more seasoned salespeople in your office. Then you get the opportunity to move to another state that's closer to some of your family or maybe a friend. This is an opportunity to live rent-free and pay off your debts, vehicle, etc. It's a big city with many more opportunities. How exciting! What opportunities may await you there? So you make the big move and continue working in insurance. You really like insurance sales, and you are hired on with a top-three insurance company this time. Finally, you are proud to work somewhere. You plug along there, and you are very successful. You're in the top five of sales leaders, and you're making almost as much money as a nurse, even buying your first home.

One day a customer presents another opportunity for you that you didn't even know existed. She is a branch manager of a mortgage company and wants to talk to you about a loan officer position she has available. Eventually, she hires you, even though you have no experience! Starting the second year, you are making twice as much as a nurse's salary and more money than you ever thought you'd see in your career, maybe even your lifetime! How differently your life turned out with just a few different choices. However, it's important to take note again that it's not about the money and that this can be a major distraction from God. You must be careful when climbing the ladder of success. The love of money usually means long hours, being tired all the time, new temptations, and less time for God, family, and friends. Success and our identity in that success can become our god and idol, which is a sin. The moral of the story is that life can change in an instant and that one job can build on and prepare you for the next. Take time to stop and smell the roses and make sure your train hasn't come off the rails. Step back and remind yourself where you came from, and steer clear of a prideful heart.

When you start to look for options on career choices, consider applying for work through different staffing companies. First, these type companies call on hundreds of businesses all around the city every month. They offer all types of work, including clerical, skilled labor, warehouse workers, positions that require college degrees, executive assistants, engineers, and the list goes on and on. It could be temporary or permanent. And what exactly is "temp to hire?" You are hired for the position on a trial basis, usually for ninety days (temporary) of proven performance before you are offered a permanent position with the company and offered full benefits. Another positive to this option with the staffing company is that you can work for multiple employers and see differences in companies, management, training, and job positions. This gives you a chance to experience different types of work and help you determine what type of position you feel more comfortable in. When considering this option, be sure to narrow your field down to only a few job options. With too many jobs on your resume, you may seem unsettled, that you don't want to work, or that you don't get along with people well. There are so many businesses that are unseen by the everyday public, and they may offer you skills and training for positions you haven't even heard of. Because the staffing agency has connections with so many of these contacts, that's a definite advantage for you.

Second, some employers will give you a test before agreeing to hire you on to work. These are not like school tests. These test your personality or morality. You may often get an opportunity for a job you had never considered before. Your test scores reflect how well suited you are for this field of work. This is also the case with some military jobs, and if you test well, you could climb the ladder to a top clearance and top-paying position that would be a dream job.

Third, as an option, you can try to shadow someone. You could call a business you are interested in and tell the manager you have graduated high school and that are exploring options and opportunities in that field of work. You can ask if they would allow you the opportunity to come to their office or business and shadow the person in the position that you want to know more about. You may have family friends or members of your church who would be happy for you to shadow them, and it could also help them out. Thinking about who you know is the best place to begin.

Ladies and gentlemen, there is a fourth option, and it's called skilled labor. Construction workers of all types, diesel mechanics, and CDL truck drivers are always needed. Many places also need machinists, welders, upholsterers, and furniture workers. Skilled labor can be very expensive when calling someone out to your house, especially for "honey do's." Some professionals will only want to take bigger jobs. You are paying for their skill, training, and time. Both men and women can learn the basics of painting, carpenter, plumbing, and electric work, and you would save yourselves a ton on labor cost and even some headaches caused by "shade tree" entrepreneurs, which refers to people who work under the shade of trees in their yards in their spare time.

Why pay someone else to do it, if you can do it yourself in ten or fifteen minutes? Grab on to someone's back pocket on the weekends, and volunteer to be their helper for the day. Ask these people to show you how they did something, and try it yourself. You are offering free labor for the opportunity to learn some of those skills. (Yes, girls, you can do this too.)

Here are some examples of the annual salaries for skilled jobs from Salary.com (in Jackson, Mississippi):

1. Construction manager: $95,765.00
2. Diesel mechanic: $53,277.00
3. CDL truck driver: $43,345.00
4. Machinist I: $42,468.00
5. Welder II: $44,758.00

6. Upholstery furniture: $50,740.00
7. Furniture/cabinet maker: $48,250.00
8. Plumber: $55,388.00
9. Electrician II: $58,249.00
10. Painter II: $48,917.00
11. Hairdresser: $26,171.00
12. Insurance sales: $55,812.00
13. Real estate agent: $41,163.00

There are other examples, but this should give you a good idea of the kind of money you could expect to make in some professions. Keep in mind that if your skills are above average, you can expect to make even more. Along with a good job and more money in your pocket comes added responsibilities. How you use those resources can affect others too. We will discuss this and more in other chapters.

Tips for College-Bound

If you haven't already started the process of researching colleges, you can start with the university or junior college you're considering attending. Does this school offer an accredited course for you to sit for the required exam? Do your credits transfer to most four-year universities if you change schools or majors? How much money is it going to cost you to go to school, and will you have to pay up front? You will have these and many other questions as you move toward the time to start classes. In this section we will look at some of the possible options and added costs.

When looking at different schools, look at the cost for each semester or year, and write it down to begin to count your cost of going there. You will also need to include the cost of housing and food if you choose to live in the dorms on campus. Subtract any scholarship money from your total, and you will be left with the amount you need to consider borrowing. Before you ever apply for your first loan, apply for the free grants first. If you qualify, this is free money for school that you don't have to pay back to anyone. Next, subtract your grant money, and that will tell you how much in financial aid you will need. Your lowest interest rates are going to be on the government-funded loans. This is also going to be your lowest payment, and your payments are deferred for a certain amount of time after you get out of school. If you are enrolled in school, they are deferred, and you won't have to start repayment on them. After financial aid, you can apply for student loans and parent plus loans for more funding. As a last resort, you can take out a personal loan through a bank. That would mean a very high interest rate, and you would have a payment monthly starting after the first month you accept the loan. This option should only be used as a last resort to pay for any schooling. Please set up a meeting with your admissions counselors, and they can guide you and give you all the information on what money you will need for school.

Okay, so you have your school paperwork for the fall semester. You've picked your classes, and you've applied for student loans and/or grants. Now what?

Apartment Living

If you have chosen an apartment, you will need more items than a dorm. You can purchase many of these items at garage sales.

Start thinking about this now and go out early on Saturday morning's so that you can get the good stuff. You can find gently used items you will need for very little cost. By starting out early, you can take your time and really find some diamonds in the rough. You should know your living arrangements by now and can determine how much room you will have to work with. Be careful not to overbuy. Remember you will be moving this again and again and again. Just get your main essentials. Think about your bedding, lamps, small desk, chair, toiletries, cleaning supplies, towels and washcloths, shower curtain, paper plates and cups, a few glass plates and bowls, and pots and pans. Of course, not all of these will come from garage sales. Your parents may give you some of these.

Think about your necessities. You do not have to start off having everything right now! You don't have to have a full living room set, dining room set, wall art, or a cabinet full of china. Hold off on some of these things until you can be sure you are going to settle in that city or town and/or until you have a place of your own. Then you can start collecting your nicer pieces little by little as you go.

In an apartment, not only will you have a bigger and nicer space, but you will be heads and tails ahead of your peers when it comes to learning life skills and handling all your bills.

> And my God will provide every need of yours according to his riches in glory in Christ Jesus (Philippians 4:9 NIV).

Dorm Life

If you are living on campus, don't procrastinate about turning in your important paperwork! One day past the due date is too late, and you will be stuck with what the school chooses for you. You will hear a voice echoing in the back of your mind, repeating, "You get what you get, and you won't throw a fit." If you have chosen a dorm, that is great! Let's look at some pros and cons to the dormitory environment. With the community of a dorm, you can meet people and connect with someone you really like, and then you could make a good friend for life. However, this could be a con if you are an introvert and like to keep to yourself and don't care for a lot of people around. You can always close yourself up in your room. But you will have a roommate, and then there are people next door with whom you share a wall. One plus is that you don't have to worry about sending off five different bills because it's all included with your tuition and is already taken care of. Some other positives to living in a dorm is that you are right on campus and close to everything. You won't have a whole lot of space in the dorm room itself, so you will not be spending money on a bunch of furniture and items to fill it up. This is money that you can save for later when you do have your own place. You will have a universal kitchen and laundry in the building that everyone shares along with a lounge area and study rooms. So this could become a challenge, especially since you have to share the kitchen and laundry room with so many hands. You will need to coordinate your time or plan on taking your clothes home on the weekends. Another con is that the air and heat for the whole building is controlled by a central monitor not in the building, and when it breaks, you must send a request for the repair, which could take quite some time to process. Keep in mind that these buildings are sometimes old and can have quirks and issues. With that in mind, you may need to keep an extra clean room to keep the bugs out of it. Welcome to dorm life. Hello, real world!

Home Life

If you choose to live at home, this is a great opportunity for you to save to pay on school or use your savings as an emergency fund. Try to put some money away and save, save, save. There is an emphasis on the word opportunity here! You have this awesome opportunity to save, so don't regret wasting this time with shopping sprees and toys. Condition yourself to make a habit out of putting away little by little. You may not even be considering the thought of saving, and that is the very reason you need to have it on your mind. At this age you really don't see and understand how important this will be later in life and the benefits of it. The Bible talks a lot about money and how it can lead you down a slippery slope. It's not the money that is the problem. It's the steward of the money and how we handle and use it. You've probably heard the saying "It's not the machine. It's the operator." Yep, here's your sign! Money isn't evil in itself. It's the love of money and how you spend it that creates issues.

When you live at home, you will have to think about the money you will spend on extra gas. Also, another con could be that you are paying for your food in the cafeteria and in off-campus eateries if you get hungry. It's not likely you can drive home and make a sandwich. One way to save money on food is to bring a sack lunch or a snack with you instead of eating out all the time. You can even go back to your vehicle to eat it. Thinking about your study group time, you have the option to FaceTime or Skype with your classmates if you can't always meet face to face. There are always solutions to the logistics you will have to navigate when you are living at home.

Supplies

Let's talk about your class supplies (notebooks, pens, etc.). Think about Walmart or Office Depot and their "back to school" sales in August. However, you shouldn't go in August. You will need to go around October for the sales or before August when stores run specials. After the season you can go straight to the clearance aisle where they have everything marked down significantly. The items may include anything from dry-erase boards, and notebooks to book covers, pencils, and glue sticks. This is the time to stock up! You don't want to skimp on the amount you purchase, or you will kick yourself for not getting another one of something. Think about the following semesters, and buy enough to stockpile some for later.

Be sure to have a great calculator. You will be using it all the time. Ask some of your friends who have taken the same classes you are going to be in for their opinions, or ask the professors what type of calculator is going to benefit you the most in their classes and in future classes. When it comes to buying your study books, it's time to really think outside the box. Ask friends, friends of friends, classmates, and/or teachers about needing a new book. Can you buy it used? Go straight to the professor, and ask if a previous edition will work or if you will even really need the book! Try to avoid the campus bookstore. You will spend way more there than any other place. Look around, and shop off campus or online. Go to bookstores with used books for sale. Call around before you go to save yourself some time and unnecessary work. Did you know that you can even rent your books? Ask for help. Seriously, ask, ask, ask! This is only going to benefit you!

What about free? Check out your local library for that exact book. You may be nicely surprised, and it's only going to cost you the library membership and rental fees. There are multiple sites where you can find books, but how do you know which one is the best? Word of mouth can provide the best information, and there are several tried and true sites that past students have used for their books. Check out cheapesttextbooks.com. They'll search the internet for you. The search engine will give you multiple vendors with their prices of the books too. Even try sites like Amazon and Chegg, and then search for apps from some of the major chain bookstores. These apps offer coupons, promo codes, discounts, and sales if you sign up as a member with them. Don't forget to ask friends or acquaintances who have had that class. They may still have their books, and they may lend them to you or sell them to you cheap!

So which is going to be the best option? It's going to come down to researching all the tools available. Isn't it worth it if it can save you several hundred or thousand dollars a semester? You can also look forward to selling your books to someone else at the end of the semester. You can recoup some of your expenses and end up with extra pocket change you didn't count on. Where do you sell them though? I'm so glad you asked! You're going to go to one of the same places, but mostly online and the bookstores. You may even walk away with more money than you paid in the first place for the book!

Campus Activities and Free Food

> **"** Here's a reminder: Don't forget to take advantage of the free activities on your campus. **"**

On campus there will be lots of opportunities available to meet new people and eat all kinds of free food. Networking opportunities are all around you. You can expand your connections and be more in the know about campus activities! And did I say free food? Take advantage of as much as you can without overloading yourself by being too involved. Fraternities and sororities are known for having weekend bashes, and they often provide food and snacks. Some of these are exclusive to the members, but you can just walk right up to some and explore the houses and use this opportunity to meet new people. Check bulletin boards, flyers, the school website, and social media. Read them! Get involved! You will never get to experience these opportunities again.

There are always tailgating opportunities and football games to go to. Even if you're not a huge fan, they are much more fun than you remember in high school. Then you may consider a different kind of opportunity. Each school has lots of organizations that have positions to fill every semester (president, vice president, secretary, treasurer, etc.). Even the school newspaper fills positions for school reporters. If you'd like to get involved and be in the know, just ask how you can volunteer or how you can plug in

> **"** A good thing to remember is that the title of the school doesn't matter. What matters is applying yourself fully and taking advantage of all the chances you have while you are there. **"**

more on campus to help. Try out for dance team or an activity like this. Now is the time to be adventurous and try something you didn't think you could in high school.

In the Beginning

Everyone is in the same boat as you are, and you are all starting with a huge learning curve. Sure, you are all going to be a little nervous, a little scared, and unsure of yourselves. Just remember you are not alone. You are not the only one experiencing these feelings.

 The older you get, the more people you meet with the same insecurities, health problems, and struggles. God will put those souls in your path at just the perfect time to be of comfort to you. **"**

This is the perfect time to reinvent yourself! I'm not talking about a new you or a fake you. I'm talking about other people's perceptions of you. This is a fresh start and a chance to make things right. You can create an environment you can thrive in, so take full advantage of this chance! If you have been waiting to step out of your shell or not feel stuck under the cloud that covered you in high school, go for it! If you think you're labeled loser, geek, dumb jock, or shy, this is your time to show the world what you are really made of and what accomplishments you can achieve when you put your mind to something. Talk to people you are afraid to talk to. They are just as afraid to talk to you too! You can have the same misperceptions about others as they have about you. You will be surprised once you start stepping out of your comfort zone and engaging in new conversations.

Step out of your comfort zone when making class choices, and choose electives and classes that you would be interested in learning or knowing more about. Be sure to take that extra language, art, or music class. There are so many opportunities for bilingual translators, and companies will consider you a valued employee if you can expand their footprint and product to other markets in other countries. That additional skill can complement your resume for the wow factor. Give them the chocolate-covered sundae with nuts, whipped topping, and a cherry rather than a vanilla cone.

Response and Responsibility

H as a friend or family member ever told you that you were irresponsible? It really hurts your feelings, doesn't it? Even though you try to let it roll off your back, it really stings for a while.

Imagine hearing these words from secondhand sources: "They are not very mature, are they?" Ouch! That can really hurt and shock you! Why would they say that? They are supposed to be your friends, and true friends wouldn't do that, would they? They are always so sweet and respectful when you're around them. You say to yourself, "I'm mature. I'm responsible. I've paid for my car all on my own. I pay rent, electric bills, and phone bills, and I live on my own. How can they say that? Where is that even coming from? Did I do something that was immature in front of them?"

They could be seeing something from the outside that you are totally blind to. Yes, it hurts, and you don't want to hear it, much less believe it. But trust that this is coming from something they have seen in you and should be taken as a reality check. Take what they say to heart, and use it as motivation to try to find out why they said what they did. If we are never told that we are behaving a certain way, we may never notice it, and we may never have the opportunity to correct the behavior before it becomes a bad habit. Use this as a learning experience and don't get puffed up with pride or arrogance. Pride comes before a fall. None of us are ever too good to take constructive criticism and definitely not when we are still wet behind the ears! You may have to google that saying.

When people are trying to tell you something, don't be so hardheaded that you can't even be open to the possibility of exploring how you could do a better job in this area. "Just wait a minute," you say. "I didn't do anything wrong!" It may be that is your personality and that you were just having fun. However, since you can't be a fly on the wall, you may just ask a few other people's opinions or ask someone you trust to be truthful with you.

> 66 Sometimes we don't see the forest for the trees. 99

"When I was a child, I used to speak like a child, think like a child, reason like a child; when I became a man, I did away with childish things" (1 Corinthians 13:11 NIV).

You may not care what people think of you, and you may not even care if they talk about you, but what you do need to care about is how you respond to criticism. Only you can control what comes out of your mouth, and once you say it, you can't take it back. It's much easier to say it right or hold your tongue to begin with instead of feeling guilty and asking for forgiveness later. You don't have control over what other people do or say. You only have control over one person—yourself.

"Whoever would love life and see good days, must keep their tongues from evil and their lips from deceitful speech" (1 Peter 3:10 NIV).

If you would like your life to feel easier and experience more guilt-free days, trust me. Less is more. Our tongues can get us into a whole heap of trouble. The less we say, the better off we usually are. Sometimes it's not at all what we think, and we may just find out later that if we had opened our mouths, then we would have been really embarrassed. Is what you have to say worth losing a relationship over?

There are many different ways people can respond to one another. Be mindful of your thoughts, before they come out in word form. Pay close attention to godly people and people you respect. Listen to their words, and take note of their demeanor. How did people respond to them? Watch and learn from healthy families and their example. The healthier we are mentally, the healthier the people in our sphere of influence become.

Responsibility—and how we handle that responsibility—is vital to our testimony as Christians and the influence we have on others. Habits you create now, however small, will probably end up impacting your professional career as well. Employers are now factoring in social media posts in their hiring decisions. If they see your social media littered with profanity, questionable content, or unethical behavior, then they are going to steer clear of you. You are a lawsuit just waiting to happen.

> **66** Think twice, post once. Do you want to be respected and known as a loyal, honest, and dedicated employee whose value is above any of their coworkers or someone who's lazy, undependable, unethical, and easily replaceable? **99**

What about your response to friends and family members who give unsolicited advice? They often give advice whether you want it or not. They can have demeaning attitudes and end up discouraging your hopes and dreams. This feeling is quite disheartening when it comes from your own family, the ones you thought would support you through thick and thin. You can't understand how this person you have known all your life would lose faith in you so quickly. However, as you get older, you will learn this is more of the norm than the exception. Turn this into a positive, and let this experience help you grow thicker skin so that you can deal with negativity. Try to consider what you could say in those situations and when to say nothing at all.

This behavior can tear down your self-esteem, making you doubt your abilities, and it will also deflate your drive to apply your God-given talents and motivation. As a result, you may miss a great opportunity and a possible stepping stone toward your career goals. It could even be a path God wants you to pursue. You will find that it is much better to pray and discern how God is leading you than to listen to worldly wisdom and jeopardize God's blessings for you anyway. If something feels forced or chaotic, it's usually not from God. Remind yourself to be still in order to hear God, and He will give you peace about your decisions and will show you a clear path. If it is not of God, there will be chaos around, and you will not be settled on any one thing.

Sticking to your guns and having confidence in yourself is an admirable quality in life, but don't be too stubborn just because you are trying to prove a point. Only you know just how much you are capable of. No one else does. Take that first step of faith and believe in God for strength and wisdom. Remember to be still for a while so that you can hear Him and His will for you.

> **66** Charles R. Swindoll said, "We cannot change our past ... we cannot change the fact that people will act in a certain way. We cannot change the inevitable. The only thing we can do is play on the one string we have, and that is our attitude. I am convinced that life is 10% what happens to me and 90% of how I react to it." And so it is with you. We are in charge of our attitudes. **99**

Decisions, Decisions, Decisions

Part of responsibility is making good decisions and your attitude about those. You will have to make a decision about your living arrangements, namely if you will stay at home or live away from home. You could live in a dorm with a roommate or an apartment. If you need a roommate to help cut your costs, who are you going to choose? You probably want a friend who you trust, but you don't always have that option. Besides, that's not always your best option anyway, even if you think it is right now. Too much togetherness can stress friendships, and then you wind up ruining a friendship. It's not worth losing a friend over, and you know you will be together a lot anyway. Someone you don't know or an acquaintance could be a good option for you, and the person could end up being the best roommate ever! What about someone you work with or friend of a friend? From experience, you shouldn't rush into finding someone. If you are stuck in a panic and must find someone at the last minute when your rent is due, you may have to choose someone you don't know and may not trust. Of course, how much do you really know about anyone until you live with that person? You really find out about people when you are sharing a space with them. Everyone was raised differently, and we all have different routines. Just because something is normal to them and not to you, that doesn't mean it's wrong necessarily. It just means it's different. Looking at differences this way will help you get along better.

Words of Caution

Some friends are going to take advantage of you, steal from you, stress you out, and leave you in a bind. Not everyone is going to do laundry the way you do or clean up after themselves. You learned how to cook, but they may not cook at all. Do your potential roommates like peace and quiet or do they like to party? Are they early birds or night owls? Do they have company over like a boyfriend or girlfriend staying the night? Even if they say nothing is going on, their behavior could be damaging to your testimony as a Christian. People will talk, so remember that someone is always watching and will inevitably see your actions. How can you be a good witness for the Lord if your peers think you are just like these roommates living in the secular world. These are all things you must take into consideration if you want to live a life upright and honorable before the Lord.

Be extra careful if you keep cash or jewelry at home. If you hide the cash in a pillowcase, in the freezer, or under the mattress, someone will find it.. If people want to get to your money or anything else, they are going to find a way to do it. Do not be naïve about people's intentions. Be proactive about taking appropriate Be proactive, and always be aware of what is going on around you. precautions upfront to protect yourself. Guard yourself against losing valuables and winding up with a broken heart in the process. Roommate relationships can grow if you cover all the important information up front and communicate with each other on any possible issues before they become problems.

A Proactive Life

Learning to be proactive in life helps prepare you for what is to come and will lessen the surprises of life. You should think about the possible outcomes of your choices and the actions you will need to take. A proactive person tends to be a good problem solver. For example, if your vehicle is getting older and needs minor repairs, then it's probably a good idea to start saving for any unexpected problems. You must change your oil regularly, so you should include that in your budget every three months. Do you have a savings account with two to six months of expenses saved up? This is something to work toward as you get older. This may be different for you, but it's a good idea to keep at the forefront of your mind. You will get there one step at a time.

What about when you're driving? Can you be a proactive driver? Of course you can! Leaving your home early is a perfect example of being proactive. Prepare for the unexpected on the road. While driving, you can calculate ahead of time if you need to take an alternate route, depending on how heavy the traffic is. Expect the unexpected, and you will never be surprised.

Being goal-oriented in life is part of being proactive. How will you ever achieve any of your goals if you are not aiming for them? Write down your goals and dreams. There is something about putting these goals on paper and seeing the pros and cons side by side. Look at what you write in different categories, and decide which ones are more realistic. Which goals can you achieve first? Does one goal build on another? Ask friends and family members what they think you are good at? This process of elimination could lead you in a direction you wouldn't have expected or seen had you not asked someone to help you. This is a great way to be proactive with your future! Start writing a to-do list every day. You will be surprised by how much you accomplish and how much more time you have for other things.

For roommate preparation and screening, here are some examples of important questions:

1. How are you and your roommate going to split the bills? Who will be in charge of paying what?

2. What are the rules about houseguests, cooking, cleaning, using the other roommate's personal items, and what's expected when washing and drying clothes. You will inevitably fight over somebody's clothes not being taken out of the dryer and/or the washer.

3. What are the rules about picking up after ourselves or taking out the garbage? Some people are very lazy, and it's a great idea to lay out some ground rules and schedules up front.

> **"** It is much easier to ask all the hard questions at the start than to get into a fight because you never discussed these items. **"**

> **"** Consider shopping for groceries together. That way neither of you will feel that you are spending more than the other person, and both parties are accountable. **"**

4. Whose name will the utilities be listed under? This is a toss-up. It could be beneficial to put everything in one person's name, or you could split the utilities between the two of your names. Either way, if someone moves out, the other person is going to have to change over utilities into their name. Don't forget about deposits! If you have a good credit score, the deposits could be lower or even zero. With a lower credit score, your deposit may come to several hundred dollars. (There's more information on credit scores in another chapter.)

5. How is the apartment or dorm going to be furnished? Do you and your roommate both have pieces of furniture? Are your parents giving or buying pieces for you? What is your roommate's style?

Budgeting and Money and Stewardship

As stewards of money, we are not the true owners of that money. We are just overseeing it for God. God made the whole world, and He owns everything in it, including money. He gives it to us, and He can take it away from us. Read over the

> **Without council plans fail, but with many advisors they succeed (Proverbs 15:22 NIV).**

parable of the talents when you have a few minutes (see Matthew 25:14–30 and Luke 19:12–27 NIV).

God tells us through Luke's account that if we can be trusted with very little, then we can also be trusted with a lot. He also lets us know that if we are dishonest in our dealings with our money, sin is going to grow, and we will be dishonest in a lot. We also see from this scripture that we are to be fruitful and use the resources God has provided to us. When you are a poor college student starting out, you rely on the kindness of your Christian brothers and sisters to donate and help support you with their gifts. You also depend on the continued support of your parents and family. You are blessed because others chose to bless you from their abundance and fruitfulness. Therefore, we all need to have the mind-set of Christ when it comes to meeting one another's needs and blessing others. As others bless us, we in turn can also bless other people. It is more blessed to give than to receive. The Bible tells us that we are the ones who get the blessing if we give to others. Allow others to bless you in your time of need, and then you can do the same for someone when you are able.

If others have blessed you, God will give you the opportunity to return that blessing to them or pass it on to someone else. What comes around goes around, right? The Bible talks about how the Christians pooled all their resources together, and because of this, every single one of them had exactly what they needed, and no one was lacking in anything. With Jesus as their teacher, they were able to model the premise of sharing. Essentially, if you share, others will likewise share with you.

Credit Cards

First, everyone needs at least one revolving credit card. Credit cards are different from a bank card linked to your checking account. You use these to build your credit and to charge items on occasionally. Debit cards are not reported on your credit. Nor do they build your credit score. Apply for a simple student visa or even a popular retail/grocery store card that will report your purchase history to your credit bureau. You want a card that will report to the credit bureau. Clothing store cards and gas cards will get you in trouble because it's tempting to use these all the time. Get a card you know you will only use periodically to help build your credit score. Be sure there are no hidden annual fees. To build your credit, only make purchases up to 30 percent of the credit limit. For example, if your limit is $300, charge up to $90.00 but not more than that. Sometimes you must charge more, but use this as a rule of thumb. When the credit bureau's algorithm considers its variables, this behavior is one of the factors they use in determining your credit score. Another factor will be length of time you have had that card opened. The longer you keep your card in good standing, the better your score will get. Pay them on time! You don't want to keep paying interest plus an additional late fee. So too, if you are thirty days or more past the due date, the creditor will report the late payment to the credit bureau, and that dings your credit score as a result.

Speaking of bringing your credit score down, you never want to close your credit cards. This is a big no-no, and it could take up to fifty points off your credit score. It will drop like a rock! When you buy a car or furniture or when you get a secured or unsecured loan, these are considered installment loans. Installment loans or notes are only valid for a set period of time. For example, you could have a term of twelve months, three years, or five years. Once you pay your term out, you're paid in full, and the account is closed. Therefore, this debt is no longer reporting and not a factor for your credit score any longer. That is why revolving credit is so important. Secured loans can be secured with some type of property or even a CD; unsecured loans are basically just a signature loan you sign stating that you agree to pay it back.

Another piece of information about credit is how to keep from going into collection status. This is when you have not paid on your bill for more than 90 to 120 days. Then the creditor turns the bill over to a third party to collect the money for them. Once it's a collection, it's not going anywhere for at least seven years, maybe longer. The first twelve months of a new collection will drop your score the most.

If you're not sure who the creditor is or what the bill is for, always call and ask. Once you confirm this bill is yours, the creditor will ask you how you would like to pay. Most of the time, they will give you 25 percent off the total cost to pay in full. This option is only available on the front end before any payments. Second, they can set you up on a payment plan. Some collection agencies will want to draft the payment every month. Some will allow you to pay on time, meaning that you can pay every single month what you can afford. This payment could be as low as $25.00 per month. Trust me. If the payment is automatically drafted from your account, you will never miss it, and you will pay it off in no time.

Pinching Pennies

Couponing is one way to save big on purchases, and a variety of stores accept them. A good idea is to create a small binder with different categories for health/beauty, food, paper goods, household items, and restaurants. If you watch YouTube videos for examples on how to coupon, you will learn a lot about the how-tos. You may even learn how to get items for free. There are also many apps available with digital coupons and rewards for first-time members who sign up, so take advantage of this. Sunday papers will have the most coupons, and you can get the paper for one dollar at some locations. Some stores will offer "buy one get one free" items on certain days. Buy your items when they're on sale. Plus you may have a coupon for that same item. This is where you will get the most bang for your buck and can even stock up on that item. How much money will you really save from using coupons? A lot! Your savings could be more than 50 percent if utilizing coupons correctly.

Eating cheap is also a must on a small budget! Big-box stores have demonstrations with free samples! If you're hungry on a Saturday, you can roam around your local Sam's Club and snack as you shop. Eating out is not always going to be an option for you; however, it can be hard to cook for just one. You could eat out with a friend and split the cost of the meal, or you could head to a Mexican restaurant and order off the "single portions" menu. By the time you eat the chips and salsa, you will be full.

Always do the surveys printed on your receipts. You can even fill them out right then while you're waiting on your change so you don't forget! Some have a time limit from the date of receipt, perhaps around thirty days. You could even use the coupon that same day for your supper. Pizza rewards are easy to earn free food, and you may end up with free pizza once every two months if you order at least once a week. Other coupons for "buy one get one" could be used a different way too. Have you ever eaten with a friend, split the plate, and split the cost? Use your coupon, and you could both get your meal half off! Have you ever considered half-price appetizers for your meal? Appetizers are very filling and make great entrées. Some restaurants will allow you to upgrade these to entrées for a small fee. Salad bars can be added to an appetizer at some places, and they may only charge you for the cost to add a salad.

If you like to cook, think about cooking a pot of soup or red beans and rice that can stretch for several days. You can also freeze portions to eat at another time.

Expiration dates don't mean something is ruined and inedible. Use your judgment. Google "good through" and expiration dates for that product. You'd be surprised how long food last.

 A fun way to save is to have a Julia Child-style dinner party! Invite all your friends to make recipes they have never made or tasted. Each guest will pick a dish to make and bring. Each guest will print their recipes for the other guests to take home with them!

Your college ID is going to get you discounts all around town and even out of town. Remember this when you're out. Look for or keep an ear out for grand openings or ribbon-cutting ceremonies. These events offer free food, and some offer gift certificates to the first few customers. Did you know that if you catch a deli or bakery at closing time, you are more likely to get extra portions or even free items thrown in? Saving around holidays is easy with the extra gift cards offered from restaurants with the purchase of a certain amount. Remember to always ask for a deal or discount. Everything is negotiable! But they are not going to give it to you unless you ask for it!

Checking and Savings Accounts

That brings us to the next point. Everyone needs a checking account. A checking account not only is going to track your transactions, but most banks will keep the images of checks available online. You can print or save copies as PDFs, or the bank can print a paper statement and give you copies of all your checks, which they may or may not charge you for. Checking accounts are used in a variety of transactions, including providing proof of assets or funds to close on a loan, proof of twelve months of payments, and paper trails for CPAs. Use a checking account primarily for bills and everyday expenses. You have unlimited access to withdraw funds if you have checks and a debit card to use at ATMs. You can also use a credit card statement for a paper trail. If you ever need to show proof of paying rent or utilities for the past twelve months, this will serve as documentation. To make a credit decision, some creditors may require a copy of your bank statements to show you have assets in your account.

Be sure to read the fine print in every document, and ask plenty of questions about fees associated with the type of checking account you are considering. Some have minimum balance requirements. Some draw interest too, and some have annual fees. Consider the bank fee for withdrawing money from ATMs, which is deducted from your account on top of your withdrawal. If you withdraw from your bank's ATM, they may not charge a service fee. Nowadays you can deposit funds in a drop box after hours, and you can deposit checks through the ATM or on your smart phone. Be sure to ask about what options each bank can offer you. Some even have apps for discounts at retailers, including travel, food, and other amenities.

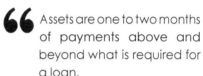

Assets are one to two months of payments above and beyond what is required for a loan.

Most asset requests are for mortgage loans in purchasing homes, but you may need assets for other reasons, including purchasing a car among others. It's a good idea to have anywhere from $1000 to $2000 in a savings account for emergencies. Emergencies will come up, and it will be a lot less stressful knowing you can take care of it instead of getting stuck in a bind. It may even be a good idea to keep this fund in a totally separate account.

Renting and Budgeting

Whether you're thinking about living alone or having a roommate, you will need to calculate your estimated bills.

Write down all expenses before jumping in. First, you want to calculate your income to see what you can afford. Start by looking at your payroll dates along with your hourly wage to estimate your average year to date income. Use the net income after taxes come out. Your overtime, bonuses, commission, or holiday pay doesn't need to be calculated into this total. If you have received an additional income for at least two years, it's likely to continue, but let's be conservative and not count this additional income.

Second, you will want to write out all your deductions from the bills you will be responsible for. Include groceries, gas, and eating out/entertainment. An overestimate is better than any underestimate of what's needed. Always do this because you could end up underestimating every month's expenses. If you are not good at math, ask someone you trust to help you the first time. Think about adding in a cushion for play money. You may like to shop or go to the movies or travel. Set aside a designated amount each month for these items. Find out from your neighbors or ask the landlord what the electric and cable bill usually runs so you will know what to estimate for these. Some rentals will include the utilities in with your rent payment.

If you need to purchase furniture, you can find cheap decor items and small furniture pieces at garage sales on a Saturday morning. You can always look at Facebook Marketplace or a thrift store (e.g. Salvation Army and Goodwill Stores). They will run specials during the week on certain days for certain items. For example, ladies clothing may be 50 percent off on Tuesdays, and all furniture may be half off every Wednesday. Some of the best deals are at garage sales. You can find lamps, curtains, clothes, and furniture pieces. Some of the best items to find at thrift shops are clothes, purses, and old dishes.

Saving Money by Living on Your Own

Let's look at ways inside your space that you can save money. One way to save is on electricity. You should always turn the lights off behind you. Don't leave inside or outside lights on all night. When it's daylight, open your curtains/blinds, and make use of the natural light. At night, turn lights off and just use the light from your TV or the light from your phone to move around. A great tip is to unplug everything that you are not currently using. If you use your TV daily, then leave this plugged in. Yes, it does make a difference. Electricity is flowing! You can also turn down your thermostat a few degrees when you leave, and that could save you 20 to 30 percent on your cooling and heating bills.

When it comes to television savings, there are many ways to cut cost. You have lots of options since there's so much competition, which can help you minimize costs and customize your experience to your specific needs. If you're not sure of the options available, google some television providers. The number of companies offering custom choices will surprise you. If you want to see how this option compares to the cable company, just give them a call, and they will gladly give you a quote over the phone. Ask them about basic coverage and what channels are included in this. They want to earn your business and will compete by offering promotions and discounts. You can also bundle several utilities together. Visit your cell phone provider, and ask them about bundling telephone, internet, and cable together for a discount. They really want your business. Therefore, they will haggle with you on price and offer any discounts or special promotions available. It's a win-win for you and them.

Make sure you have your calendar reminders set for the due dates of each bill, and list them by priority. This helps with your budgeting organization. You can also include calendar reminders for social events around campus and around town. A lot of these events will offer free appetizers, free drinks, and even coupons for free food. Include any grand openings, ribbon-cutting ceremonies, and anniversary celebrations in your social media feeds. Some retailers have special days for free drinks, free doughnuts, car wash discounts, free teeth cleanings, etc. Some churches have days they will do oil changes and give out free items to the community, mostly on Saturdays. Make sure to check local and regional websites (e.g., K-Love, Facebook, and Eventbrite) twice a week.

If you are on any medication and have to pay any out-of-pocket expenses, consider downloading the GoodRx app or applying for a discount card directly through the pharmaceutical company. This can save you 75 to 80 percent off of your prescriptions. You may need to get your pharmacist to check the price difference on different quantities. If a sixty-day supply is the same as your thirty-day supply, your doctor can write your prescriptions for a sixty-day supply instead, and it should help you save more money. This saves you not only money but also time running back and forth to the pharmacy. Create a profile, and the app will remind you when refills are due once you set it all up. With the rise of medical and prescription cost, we need every penny in savings we can get. Be sure to ask the right questions at your doctor's appointment while in his or her office. It never hurts to ask doctors about how to save money, and they may provide you with free samples or discount coupons on your prescriptions. If the pharmaceutical sales rep has left samples, they will send you home with several. It could be anything from regular prescriptions to new medicines on the market or even ointment and creams from the dermatologist.

Depending on the service received in the doctor's office or at the hospital, most medical care facilities will discount your bill if you pay in cash or pay your bill in full. Some hospitals will give you at least a 25 percent off discount if you pay the full amount of your initial bill. There is a catch though. You do have to pay up front in full before you can make any other monthly or partial payments on the account (see Cron.com).

What if you're in a situation where you need work on your vehicle? You may be in a different city or state other than your family's repair shop. You might not have any clue as to where to go or even how to start. Well, in this case, you are going to want to ask locals for referrals on who they use and what experiences they have had with that particular shop. A referral from someone at the repair shop is going to do a few things for you. First, they know if you're not satisfied with your repair, they may lose you and the customer who referred you to them. Second, dropping someone's name doesn't hurt. When you have contacts in common, this helps build a rapport with them quicker. Repair shops love repeat business, and they want you to feel comfortable coming back to them. You don't have to get all of your work done at the same repair shop though. Some shops specialize in certain repairs, and some do a better job on certain things over someone down the street. When it comes to maintenance and oil changes, there are plenty of five-minute and quick lube options that offer a student or ladies discount on certain days of the week. Some car washes offer the same type discounts. Every little bit helps, right?

Splurges

Now let's talk about splurges and how to resist temptation. You really don't need that costly mocha or hazelnut and caramel double-shot latte. Do you really have to eat out today? Why not run home and eat the leftovers in your refrigerator. They will fill you up just the same, and they are usually much healthier.

Think to yourself, *What can I buy at the grocery store for that same amount of money? Can this money pay my water bill? Is it just going to collect dust?* You can also ask yourself, "Will I ever be able to get this price on this item again? Is this a once-in-a-lifetime deal?" Let's look at a few examples.

In the case of new clothes, you can choose to pay $40 for one piece at a department store, but you can find three pieces at a garage sale for $2 each and five pieces at Goodwill for $3.50 each. That's $40 for one piece or eight pieces for $23.50. Which is the smarter buy?

Another example is that daily cup of coffee. Each one adds up! If you pay $4.50 per cup once a day for five days, a week costs you $22.50, which is half a tank of gas. That's $90.00 per month. (That could be money for your electric bill or your half of the utilities.)

Life is all about balance. Just like dieting, you need a cheat day when you can go off the diet so that you don't go totally overboard. So if you need a pick-me-up or a refresher, reward yourself with a dessert, a cup of coffee, or a new pair of shoes.

You earn the money you make, and you can allow yourself some enjoyment. The bottom line is that you should think before you spend your hard-earned money. Make it count, and make it stretch. You can always find a way to reduce your expenses.

Is Investing for Me?

First off, invest in God's kingdom, and give to Him from your firstfruits. You should give to Him before you pay for anything else. You may have never given to the church before in your life, but the Bible talks a lot about money and investing in God's church and people. You cannot out-give God. Tithing is very important to God and to the work God has chosen to accomplish. Whatever you give to the church, God will honor. Find a church you like, and consider how you can invest time and resources into helping further God's kingdom. The body of believers will invest in you and help you grow in your walk with the Lord and offer advice that money can't buy.

> 66 Bring the whole tithe into the storehouse, that there may be food in my house. Test me in this,' says the LORD Almighty, 'and see if I will not throw open the floodgates of heaven and pour out so much blessing that there will not be room enough to store it. (Malachi 3:10 NIV). 99

You can give at any age, but the Motley Fool, a popular stock adviser website, suggest as soon as possible. God promises to take care of our basic needs. Remember it is all His to begin with, and He deserves the very best stewardship for what He has given us. The parable of the talents is a great example of investing and getting a return on your money. You may or may not have been taught about the stock market, IRAs, or even annuities, but at the least you have heard of them. You don't have to be a Series 7-licensed agent to start investing into your future with just a small amount. You also don't have to be a math whiz to learn all the ins and outs of how each option works. Focus on starting and not wasting any time before you begin. You will hear middle-aged adults talk about how they wish that they would have invested way long ago or that they would have started investing when they were in college or even in their late twenties. The regrets go on and on, and they always wish they would have started earlier. Hindsight is twenty-twenty. You cannot turn back time and go back to start investing. You have lost all those years of compounded interest. This is very important for your future, and it needs to be a priority no matter what. Don't make excuses. Don't ignore the prompting of your parents, friends, or any other people who are advising you to invest right now while you are young. The Holy Spirit could be prompting them to plant that seed with you. You are always going to experience what-ifs in life, and you are always going to have regrets; however, this is one that will have a major impact on your life and your future with each year you let pass. Start small, and build from there. You must take the first step.

If you are interested in learning about some of the mechanics of managing your money better, including having an emergency fund and investing in your future, you can look for churches that offer free financial planning seminars. You can also check with other facilities that may bring in guest speakers. You will need to purchase the kit that includes your book, workbook, envelopes, among other things if you want to get the full benefit of the program. The materials are yours to keep when you leave the class, and you can listen to the CDs over and over while you are driving to and from places.

You can download the app ACORNS to save money. This particular app will round up your purchases to the next dollar amount, and this change will go toward investing in your future savings! You will never miss it! So too, if you have a job that offers a 401(k), you will want to invest up to your company match. If you leave that company, you can keep your retirement funds. You will just want to roll over your 401(k) to a private investment firm such as Morgan Stanley, Edward Jones, or T Rowe Price. This way you have an account representative that may have a local office with walk-in access. You may also be able to leave it in the same retirement fund without rolling it over, depending on your company's provider. Whatever you do, please do not cash this money out! You are going to lose half of your investment you have saved once taxes are taken out, not counting any penalties for early withdrawal. Chances are that no one is going to talk to you about these consequences ahead of time. (And besides, it's going to go in one ear and out the other.) Think about the long term. You are going to be kicking yourself once you get more versed in investing and start to see the savings you lost out on from not starting early.

Another very hard lesson to learn is the fact that money does not mix with friends and/or family! It is like oil and water, and you do not want to find this out the hard way! Believe it or not, it's true. No one can hurt you like your family. Unfortunately, we are not exposed to this until we start making money and are old enough to make decisions with this money. If you don't think friends and family members will stab you in the back, just try it and see. Everyone will say that they will pay you back.

People will make promises on the honor system, and they will break them almost every time. Do not fall into this statistic! It is not worth losing a friendship or damaging a relationship with a family member over money. Simply let it be known that you can't help them out with their situations. Offer advice, or help with solutions without it costing and hurting you. There may be a way for you to help that is not monetary in nature. If you do have the means to lend someone a hand, you may consider a compromise where you will give them the $20.00, for example, that they want to borrow, if they will cut your grass, or something along those lines. Some—though not all—will agree to do something to help you just because you are helping them. If not, you will see their true motives, which will tell how sincere they really are. If you still feel that you should give this person the benefit of the doubt and you don't receive the money back, just try to remember that it is better to give than receive. After all, maybe they just needed the money more than you did. Our God is a just God, and He will not let this sort of dishonesty go unpunished.

Working and School

Did you know that you can intern during the summer months to earn valuable experience and income? Banks will allow you to intern with them, and if you're great at your job, they will even hire you back the next year! Take advantage of these opportunities to get a feel for your career path, and ask longtime employees questions while you have their ears. There will be lots of opportunities to intern. You just must do some research and look for them.

If you are a college student, you may have access to

campus opportunities for work-study programs. Work-study is part-time work for students who qualify for financial help. This program is funded by the government and offers great experience, and you get a paycheck just like any other place of employment. There are a lot of opportunities for student jobs on campus. For those who live on campus, this is very convenient.

You may intern and decide that the atmosphere in that profession is not one that you could thrive in or that you would even be happy in. In the real world, when hiring managers are considering candidates for positions, they are not going to always look at your GPA average. They are going to look at your experience. Here is a good example: Several professions will require that you take a class or a test. You either pass or fail these tests, and they require you to at least have a score of seventy or seventy-five on average. The higher score doesn't help or hurt your hiring chances. Attorneys take the bar examination. CPAs and financial advisors may take the Series 7 exam. Insurance companies have testing for property/casualty or life and health. Mortgage companies, notaries, and the like have similar testing. Gather as much information as you can about the job to see if a certain profession is a good fit for you. The good thing about the license you may acquire is that you are not locked into one single company. Plus you can often transfer some licenses from state to state. Some companies will offer to pay or reimburse you for classes and testing fees upon completion. You will need to renew certain licenses to continue practicing in specific professions.

You can also make some extra money by volunteering to be someone's guinea pig or test subject. You can earn cash and receive discounted or free services by serving as the subject of graduate students experiments. Some dental schools offer teeth cleanings for free! Free physical therapy is another one. You may be able to get a massage or facial for twenty bucks. Some colleges will offer free health care services for enrolled students. Check out the message boards around your campuses for more opportunities.

Relationships

5

I n this chapter we will focus on all types of relationships. Some relationships will be for a season, and some will last a lifetime. Some are romantic, and some are professional. Once you get out of high school, you will begin to meet new people and experience all types of personalities and cultures from other states and countries.

Friends

Maybe you come from a small-town school where everyone knew everyone's business, or maybe you were part of a 4-A high school that graduated with more than six hundred classmates. Whatever the case, you could be coming into college with an advantage or disadvantage depending on how you look at it. As an advantage, new worlds will open up to you, and you will be able to meet people from all walks of life who come from different cities, states, and countries. On the other hand, you could see it as a disadvantage because you have not grown up around these people and know nothing about them, their morals, their ethics, and the hidden skeletons in their closet. A good rule of thumb is to be cautious and pay attention before jumping into any type of friendship.

In high school you experience many types of peer pressure involving friends. The use of alcohol, drugs, sexual activity, and social pressures are just the very tip of the iceberg. Well, not to burst your bubble, but when you get to college, some of the peer pressure will go away, and some will get way worse. Just because you were popular in high school, that doesn't mean that you are going to be all that and a bag of chips on your college campus. Some will receive reality checks, and others will receive encouragement and motivation. A former high school classmate you never associated with could become one of your closest friends. Everyone is standing at this starting line as you all move forward. Knowledge is power, and the more information you gather or the more you learn, the more options and opportunities await. Just be careful to stay true to yourself whatever you do, and stay true to what you believe in. Put God first, for that is the most important relationship in your life.

Your Relationship with God

> 66 You only have control over yourself, no one else. You can't change anyone else, but you can change yourself. Salvation comes through believing that Jesus Christ is the Son of God. Only you can choose to believe and be saved. No one else can do it for you. What are you waiting for? Please don't put off deciding. Give everything over to Christ, and allow Him to bless your life and others around you through you. 99

Out in the real world, your eyes will be opened to situations and personalities that you have not experienced before. It's also going to break your heart when you see former classmates for who they really are. Those who were popular in school will have fallen prey to the devil's schemes, and their lives will be ruined by drugs and alcohol. People you thought were one thing in high school will turn out to be something else entirely. Did they change? Or did you just open your eyes and realize your perception of them was way off base?

"Walk with the wise and become wise, for a companion of fools suffers harm" (Proverbs 13:20 NIV).

In the first ten years after graduating, you will lose several former classmates. It's sad but true. During this time in life, you will see more suicides, overdoses, and vehicle accidents. So if you find you are not enjoying the things you used to or if you are pulling away from your close friends and loved ones, please talk with people you trust and let them know what is going on inside your head. Hear out another person. You may be surprised to learn they have experienced the same thing. Don't isolate yourself for very long. You can get in your head about your situation, and this will open you up to Satan creeping in with all sorts of doubts and insecurities about things. Satan is known as the accuser and the liar. He will tell you false information, and you will doubt yourself and your friendships. Don't let him beat you down and fill your head with lies. Pray that God will cast the deception from your mind and that your eyes will be open to see clearly and trust in God to change the situation. It's all about timing. Please be patient.

Just remember that the thing that has always set you apart and will continue to set you apart is the Holy Spirit of God, not to mention your love for Him and others. You are unique. No one person is made just like you. The more you stay grounded in the Word, the more your eyes will be opened to discern and see the world around you. Look at yourself and see how God sees you. God will put the right people, scripture, or radio programs in front of you right when you need it—if you don't fight your inner voice and are open to listen. We must be willing to surrender ourselves to God's perfect will for our lives. If you don't know Christ as your personal Savior, there is hope for you. Seek Him, and you will find Him. He wants to have a relationship with you.

Let's look at a real-life story about a girl we will call

Christine. She had been to church before and had attended from age six to ten, but she wasn't a believer yet. As she grew, she learned more and more, but she still had a lot of questions. After moving with her family at ten years old, her mom stopped going to church and stopped bringing her and her sister to any church services. As time went by, Christine found herself loving more of the world than taking time to think about the Bible and the questions she once had. The devil deceived her, and her head was all jumbled with her desires and everyday life. She doubted the reality of what she had once experienced. She thought that if she didn't read the Bible, it was like it never happened, and if she didn't know what scripture said, she didn't have to pay attention to it or do what God said. That was really her thought process. She didn't want to see or read what the Bible said. She just figured that she could ignore it and that it would go away then. There was still a small voice in the back of her head telling her to remember a scripture she once read about how no one is without an excuse. No one is held blameless in the end. It was just like the times when her mom would tell her not to do something but she would do them anyway, knowing that she was wrong for her actions and that there would be consequences if her mom found out.

What Christine didn't know at the time was that no matter what she did, no matter what she knew or didn't know, she couldn't just bury her head in the sand.

Romans 1:18–33 (NIV) says,

The wrath of God is being revealed from heaven against all ungodliness and wickedness of people, who suppress the truth with their wickedness, since what may be known about God is plain to them, because God has made it plain to them. For since the creation of the world, God's invisible qualities—his eternal power and divine nature—have been clearly seen, being understood by what has been made, so that people are without excuse. For although they knew God, they neither glorified him as God, nor gave thanks to him, but their thinking became futile and their foolish hearts were darkened. Although they claim to be wise, they became fools and exchanged the glory of the immortal God for images made to look like a mortal human being, and birds and animals and reptiles. Therefore, God gave them over to the sinful desires of their hearts to sexual impurity for the degrading of their bodies with one another. They exchanged the truth about God for a lie, and worshipped and served created things rather than the creator— who is forever praised. Amen. Because of this, God gave them over to shameful lust, even their women exchanged natural sexual relations for unnatural ones. In the same way, men also abandoned natural relations with women and were inflamed with lust for one another. Men committed shameful acts with other men, and received in themselves the due penalty for their error. Furthermore, just as they did not think it worthwhile to retain the knowledge of God, so God gave them over to a depraved mind, so they do what ought not to be done. They have become filled with every kind of wickedness, greed and depravity. They are full of envy, murder, strife, deceit and malice. They are gossips, slanderers, God-haters, insolent, arrogant and boastful; they invent ways of doing evil; they disobey their parents; they have no understanding, no fidelity, no love, no mercy. Although, they know God's righteous decree that those who do such things deserve death, they not only continue to do these very things, but also approve of those who practice them.

There is good news in 1 John 5:1–5 (NIV), which says,

Everyone who believes that Jesus is the Christ is born of God, and everyone who loves the father, loves his child as well. Our fruits show our love for God: by loving others and keeping His commandments. In fact, this is what Love for God is: to keep his commands, because his commands are not burdensome, for everyone born of God overcomes the world. This is the victory that has overcome the world, even our faith. Who is it that overcomes the world? Only the one that believes Jesus is the Son of God.

The end of the story is a great one for you and Christine. She listened to God's calling and asked a coworker how to read the Bible. The coworker would read hers every night. After going to church with her coworker for about a year, Christine accepted Christ as her Savior and was baptized. Christine's mom came to her baptism that day and has continued to go to the same church ever since. You can experience the same promise and security in Jesus Christ. Reach out to other Christians, and talk to them about your salvation.

Building New Friendships

Very few of you are going to have the same friends over your lifetime. This can be a hard pill to swallow right now, but while it's hard to believe, facts are facts. Relationships can become complicated. Your friendships are going to be tested, and you will learn just what true friendship really is by trial and error. Enjoy making new friends and stepping out of your comfort zone so that you can meet new people. You don't have to share your whole life story with others to get to know them. Find a common activity you both share and hang out together. Go walking together, or you can host a movie night or even a game night. You can also go to the gym. Not everyone likes to work out, and not everyone likes going to the movie theater. However, you will likely meet someone who is as motivated as you or helps keep you motivated when it comes to exercising. This may be all you have in common and all you ever do together, which is perfectly fine. The fun part is finding friends who enjoy activities you enjoy too and making friends with others who also like different types of activities. Expand your cultural experiences from what you are familiar with, and experience new things. Friends will change, but you will also change as you get older and have new experiences.

Always remember your friends who have been there for you, and show them the respect they deserve. Don't allow your attitude to isolate you. We are built for companionship. If you allow yourself to get bitter, you are going to harden your heart. You will close yourself off from the people who are your true friends, and you may make it harder on yourself to make new ones. If you are not open to seeing the good in people and giving them chances, how are you ever going to trust anyone? Have yourself a slice of humble pie, maybe even the whole pie. But humble yourself, and put others first. Think about their feelings. The Lord says in 2 Kings, "If we allow our hearts to be tender and humble ourselves, he will hear our cries." It's because of our sincerity He hears us. Be sincere in your relationships. When we have broken spirits and come to Him, He will restore His relationship with us and other broken relationships too.

More than Friends

The boyfriend-girlfriend dynamic is a whole other animal to figure out, and it can often confuse you. Some people can have questionable motives and confusing actions that really hurt your feelings. It can be a hot mess! Long-distance relationships are especially convoluted. So if you are living in a different state or city from your sweetie, you should both discuss the situation before you move. This may be the time to part ways so that you don't hold each other back, and if it's meant to be, you will find your way back to each other. Make sure you are both headed in the same direction and that you have the same goals for the future. Your current relationship may not be meant to extend until death do you part.

Anytime people maintain long-distance relationships for a long period of time, they will tend to drift away from each other. It can really take its toll on you emotionally. You may be the exception to this rule, but be prepared to remain open-minded and not get discouraged if it all falls apart on you. It may take some of you longer to figure this out. Don't look at it as the end of the world but rather as a new chapter in life, a fresh start. He or she is not the only person you are compatible with. Once you meet the one, you will wonder what you ever saw in the other person. Most of the time, it is just a fear of the unknown and being alone that affects you.

If you are currently unattached, be content with being single and undistracted. Maintain your purity during this season in life. Most of your friends are not going to be Christians. Nor will they respect your decision to be abstinent. Just because you can stay the night with someone of the opposite gender, that doesn't mean that you should. If you are dating someone, decide a specific time that you want to end the night and stick to that time. Make your date aware ahead of time that you will be heading home around a certain time frame. This way there are no preconceived notions in anyone's head about what is going to happen later that evening.

If you make them respect you and your wishes, their true colors will come shining through, and knowing their true character will make it easier to discern healthy and unhealthy relationships. They may become some of your good friends, and they will respect you if you stand your ground. Some people will just disappear, stop calling, or stop talking to you, and this is just fine. This will happen a lot, so practice saying no if they show back up. If you're a yes-man or woman, others will likely take advantage of you. Most guys may be willing to do things for you or invite you places, but they will have hidden motives. Guys do not waste their time with the opposite sex without ulterior motives, not all the time but a lot of the time. Their motives could be pure, so give them the benefit of the doubt and get to know them better as friends. You will need to discern this for yourself, but be sure to listen to what your friends have to say about that person. If your friends see any red flags, tell them to let you know as soon as they see them, and ask them to help hold you accountable like you will for them. Someone must look out for you and your best interests. You are not always going to be your best judge.

Girls who chase boys can be just as manipulative if not more so than boys. Some girls will want to use you or take advantage of your kindness while politely draining your pocketbook. Others will need your muscles to move something or your skills as a handyman. But guys, we really do need your help because girls can't do it all by themselves.

Ladies with insecurities may just want to look good and hang out with a good-looking guy. Be honest with yourselves. We have all done these things. Please don't be this person and do this to someone else. Remember to do unto others as you would have them do to you. What goes around does come back around. It only takes one person to change one's worldly ways, and if all of us reading this book chose to be honest and do a better job at these things, we would all see a major shift in our relationships and in society. This attitude and influence would rub off on each person around us.

You will likely forget college and high school dates, and they will become distant memories. Of course, they are important, but they are part of your past. They are stepping stones, learning experiences in your life. Make these good memories and take lots of pictures as you go. You will want to remember the experiences you had—the good, the bad, and the ugly. Someday you may not remember, and when you look back at those pictures, they will remind you of all the struggles and all the fun times too. Just remind yourself that these *memories* are your past and that you have grown and moved on from those experiences.

Here's some additional advice on dating. While dating around, be careful not to date two people within the same circle of friends. Don't go out on a date or mess around with your circle of friends if you have already gone out with someone else in this circle. It can get messy. It's a big no-no, and it will cause a whole host of issues if you go out with one your good friend's ex-boyfriend. I'm not sure if you've experienced this yet, but you don't want this heartbreak and the stress it is going to cause you and your friend.

People love to talk about other people's lives, and unfortunately, this only shows one side of the story. Be 100 percent sure about your choices, and weigh your options before making a move. Seek wise counsel, not from someone who is going to sugarcoat the truth or tell you what you want to hear but from someone who has a healthy relationship. Before you decide to date anyone, talk for a period as friends. Then you can decide if you want to take it to the next level and go on a date. You waste a lot less time by not getting to know these people as friends at the start. (Have you ever noticed it seems like it takes a good four to six months to get to know people and start seeing their true selves? It's weird how that works!)

So too, if you date this way, you are less likely to get into an awkward situation with someone you don't know. Think outside the dating box. For example, instead of going on a blind date, you could bring your friend with you or go on a double date with someone. You can get into some hairy or bad situations that could destroy your name and reputation. It's good to have another couple there to back you up. Remember people talk, and they love to talk about what they have done to make themselves look good. You can avoid this gossip altogether when you put thought into your decisions beforehand. Don't let the what-ifs and the regrets haunt you.

Be loyal to your friends and the person you are dating. If you want to date around and not have a serious relationship, make that clear from the start. The very beginning of any relationship is the perfect time to check people out and ask them all the awkward or hard questions to get real and honest answers. You're getting to know each other, and you can really find out a lot of important information. Find out where a person really stands on God, their morals, and their upbringing. You don't want to get four to eight months down the road only to find out something that will totally call the whole deal off. Then you will have wasted those months with someone who is not a good fit and miss out on someone you were truly supposed to meet during this time. When you are not dating, take this time for personal reflection and growth. You don't need a boyfriend or girlfriend to make you happy and whole. Learn to be happy with yourself, and be content being single. If you feel as if there's something missing in your life, fill that hole with God and His Word.

New Chapter

The Next Chapter

igh school classes are not going to teach you all these things. You can't learn these skills from your parents or college. These are all topics that you need to discuss, practice, and learn. Hopefully, you will retain some of these tips. With God's discernment, this information will hopefully save you some heartache and struggles. The advice given in this chapter is from everyday people like you who have lived and learned from their mistakes. They can look back and think about what was important and the sound advice they would now give. Listen to what these people had to say when I asked them what they might want to do differently and what advice they would give their younger selves if you could do it all over again. Some are going through their first, second, or fourth year in college, and others have already earned their degrees.

Kimberly Reed

1. "Life isn't much different just because you graduate high school. My college, Hinds, was like the thirteenth grade. Ha-ha! I was still living at home, going to school, and working. But my parents still had expectations of me. It wasn't the big 'Wow, I'm an adult' as I thought it would be.
2. "It's not about the number of friends you have, but the quality of friends. Keep your circle small and filled with people who have the same goals you do."

Heather Kuriger

1. "Okay, for me, getting out of high school was the absolute best. I moved away and got to be who I wanted

to be and got a fresh start. I learned not to let other people determine who you are, but you decide who you want to be."

2. "I wish I would have known not to rush that time but to enjoy every second and to take bigger risk."

Anonymous

1. "I wish I would have gotten better counsel on other opportunities or options to consider. And to not party so hard and take studying more seriously, to make better grades."

Anonymous

1. "I wish I would have studied the Bible more and known more of what to do and what not to do as far as right and wrong."

Tyler Johnson

1. "Do not let anyone tell you that you can't do anything. You can do anything you set your mind to. Follow your heart, and you will succeed.

Maggie Bowman

1. "Friends are vital. But some are not permanent, and that's okay."

2. "Find a college ministry where you can grow and fellowship with people like you."

Taylor Outlaw

1. "Don't let other people's opinions hold you back from who you are because in the end, your opinion is the only one that matters."

Allie Massey

1. "Believe in yourself. You can do anything you set your mind to. Don't let anyone tell you otherwise, and don't settle for anything less than what you deserve."

Hunter Tucker

1. "Trust in the Lord with all your heart and lean not on your own understanding; in all your ways submit to Him, and He will make your paths straight" (Proverbs 3:5–6 NIV).

Anonymous

1. "If going to college, go wherever it's paid for."

Kaitlyn Evans

1. "It's okay to fail or make mistakes because when you do, you learn from it. Sometimes you have to fail to succeed."
2. "It's okay to not know what you want to do for the rest of your life. It's okay to change your mind a million times. Just make sure that when you figure it out, it's something that you love doing."

Jacob Watkins

1. "Do not—and I repeat—do not go into the military."

Anna Beth Bowman

1. "Just because your journey doesn't match up to all your friends doesn't mean you're failing."
2. "When you keep getting denied for opportunities, take a step back, and ask God if that's the plan He has for you instead of it being your plan."
3. "Give your worries/problems to God, and let Him fix them in *His* timing instead of you trying to fix them in *your* timing."

May you be encouraged by the words and advice you have read here. Act and utilize the tools you have been given to help ease the next several years of stress you are going to face. When faced with decisions, pray and ask God for His will and His guidance. Listed in the following pages are scriptures that may encourage you during difficult times.

- "Peace I leave with you; my peace I give to you. Not as the world gives do I give to you. Let not your hearts be troubled, neither let them be afraid" (John 14:27 ESV).
- "Create in me a clean heart, O God, and renew a right spirit within me" (Psalm 51:10 ESV).
- "Brethren, do not be children in your thinking; yet in evil be infants, but in your thinking be mature" (1 Corinthians 14:20).

- "Do not be conformed to this world, but be transformed by the renewal of your mind, that by testing you may discern what is the will of God, what is good and acceptable and perfect" (Romans 12:2).
- "Therefore, brothers, be all the more diligent to make your calling and election sure, for if you practice these qualities you will never fail" (2 Peter 1:10).
- "He heals the brokenhearted and binds up their wounds" (Psalm 147:3).
- "Therefore, accept one another, just as Christ also accepted us to the glory of God" (Romans 15:7).
- "You may make your plans, but God directs your actions" (Proverbs 16:9).
- "Whoever loves money never has enough; whoever loves wealth is never satisfied with their income. This too is meaningless" (Ecclesiastes 5:10).
- "Above all, love each other deeply, because love covers over a multitude of sins" (1 Peter 4:8).
- "Walk with the wise and become wise, for a companion of fools suffers harm" (Proverbs 13:20).
- "And God is able to bless you abundantly, so that in all things at all times, having all that you need, you will abound in every good work" (2 Corinthians 9:8).

About the Author

Stacey McCrory was born in Louisiana but raised in Mississippi. She went to college in Alabama and Mississippi, and she lived in Baton Rouge, Louisiana for 14 years. She currently teaches the college Sunday school class at her church with her husband Michael alongside of her.

Over the past seven years, she has had the privilege to teach, mentor, love, and pour into almost a hundred students. She has put on college conferences, has been an active president and secretary for a business networking group, and is actively serving at her church and in the community. Her previous work includes nine years of experience in the insurance industry and fifteen years in mortgage lending. She loves learning how to do new crafts or projects of any kind and could be an interior designer with her experience and HGTV degree, of course!

She saw a huge gap in Christian guidance and information available to help prepare the younger generation for adulthood and the real world. No one educated her during or after high school on the possibilities, the hurdles, and the information needed to be her best and to start early. It would take years to learn all this information on your own. Her heart's desire is to pour as much information as possible into the up-and-coming generations and to equip them with godly direction in their lives.

CPSIA information can be obtained
at www.ICGtesting.com
Printed in the USA
BVHW030717280719
554513BV00002B/9/P

9 781973 657644